Gabby Grape Meets Junk Food Junkie!

Gabby Grape Meets Junk Food Junkie © Copyright 2018 by Linda Hodge-McLoud and Harry McLoud

All rights reserved. No part of this book may be reproduced or transmitted in any form or by any means, electronic or mechanical, including photocopying, recording, or any information storage and retrieval system, without written permission from the author or publisher.

This book is a work of fiction. Names, characters, businesses, organizations, places, events and incidents either are the product of the author's imagination or are used fictitiously. Any resemblance to actual persons, living or dead, events or locales is entirely coincidental.

Recommended reading for children in grades 1 to 5. The story offers engaging characters, easy-to-follow plots and popular topics.

Concept: Linda B. Hodge-McLoud
Written by Linda Hodge-McLoud and
Edited by Harry H. McLoud
Cover Art and Illustrations by Cynthia Agee

Published by Prominence Publishing
www.ProminencePublishing.com

ISBN: 978-1-988925-10-3

In a small town called Healthyville, there lives a fruit called Gabby Grape. Her close friends call her GG! She is honest, brave, smart, loves to have loads of fun – and she is "very talkative"! That is why she is called "Gabby". Her mission in life is to encourage everyone - especially YOUNG CHILDREN - to eat more healthy foods like fruits, vegetables, nuts and grains and to get plenty of exercise. "This will help us all to live long, healthier lives", says Gabby.

Gabby Grape is walking over to visit her best friend, AppleLean.

She is on her cell phone texting AppleLean.

She is so busy sending text messages back and forth that she doesn't see the stranger standing in front of her.

Gabby Grape bumps right into him! "Oh, I am so sorry", says Gabby Grape. "Well, if you weren't so busy looking down at your phone, you would have seen me!" Gabby Grape stands there with her mouth wide open. She is shocked and a little embarrassed. She thinks to herself, "Just who is this guy in this ridiculous big coat anyway?"

"Forgive me if I hurt your feelings, 'Little' Grape! Let me introduce myself: my name is Junk Food Junkie and my friends The Munchies call me J." He then burst out with this really ridiculous laugh. Junk Food Junkie is wearing a baseball cap. He has on a rather large grey pinstripe suit coat.

He opens up his suit coat and it is lined with all kinds of sweet and salty snacks. There is soda pop, doughnuts and cookies hanging on the left side and on the right side there are all kinds of candy, potato chips, corn chips and more!

Junk Food Junkie is wise and charming and he is also a very sly talker which makes it very easy for him to convince others to do WHATEVER he wants them to do!

From his pocket he takes out a big chocolate chip cookie. Gabby Grape looks at it, then looks at him and says "No thanks, Junk Food Junkie.

I'm not allowed to eat sugary snacks before dinner." (You see, Gabby Grape doesn't eat a lot of junk food or unhealthy snacks. It's just the way they do things in Healthyville). "Awww, you don't eat any candy, cookies or yummy potato chips before dinner? Who made up that silly rule?" asks Junk Food Junkie. "My parents!" says Gabby Grape proudly.

"Eating a delicious chocolate chip cookie right after school is the best thing ever – even before dinner! Oh, and did I mention that it has big chunks of delicious chocolate chips? Here, taste it! You know you want to!" says Junk Food Junkie. Gabby Grape replies, "I would rather eat a delicious, juicy red apple. Have you ever heard the saying **'An apple a day keeps the doctor away'? Well, it's true!"** She hands him one.

"Apples are also a good source of fiber. They are packed with vitamin A, vitamin C, iron and they are also rich in fiber. Fiber helps you to do the 'Number Two', you know what I mean?" she says while giggling. "They actually help keep you strong and healthy so that you can do all the things you want to, like play sports and even climb apple trees. All of these things are fun ways to get plenty of exercise. (She winks) And one more thing…"

"Hey, be quiet and just give me the apple!" He takes a look at it, smells it and takes a big bite. Suddenly, his lips start to turn BLUE and they begin to swell up. "I'm feeling faint!" he yells. He starts gasping for air, twirling and swirling all around in circles. He finally spits out the apple. "You little Purple Blob! You tried to poison me!"

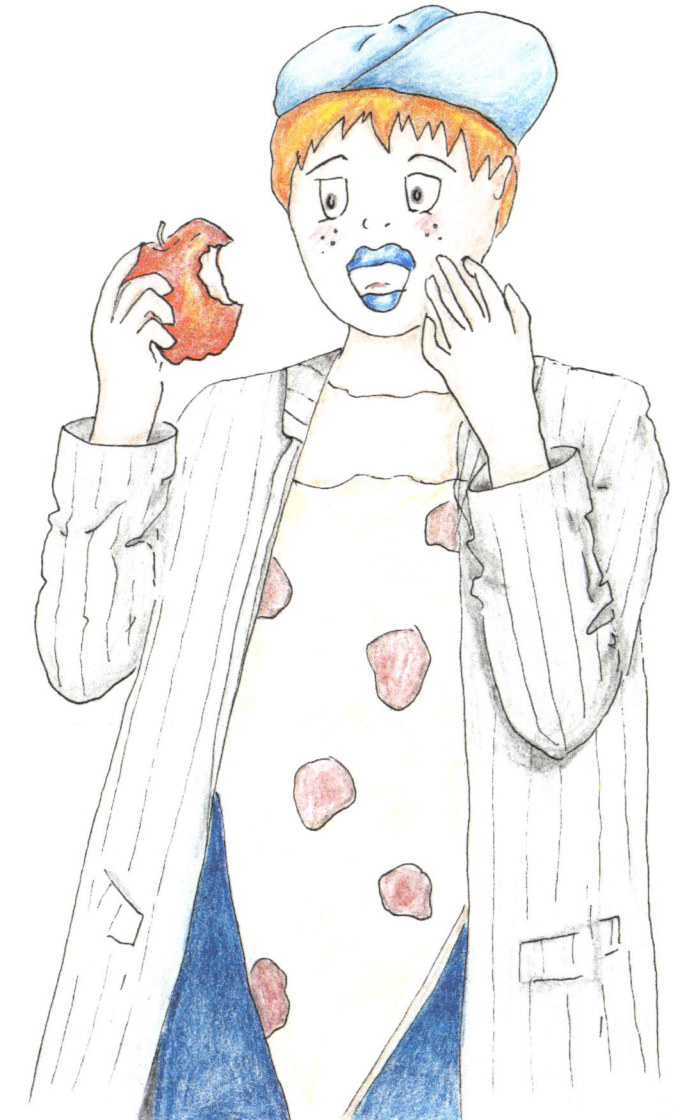

Gabby Grape laughs. "No, Junk Food Junkie! I gave you a healthier, sweet snack instead of a cookie! Now – and as I was trying to tell you earlier – remember it's important to eat plenty of fruits and vegetables every day and to get plenty of exercise by getting out and having fun! Catch you later, Strawberry!" She starts to walk away, but he steps in front of her. "Yeah, right! We will meet again, 'Little Missy'. And the next time it won't be so good for you! Ha! Ha! Ha!"

She quickly pulls out her cell phone and takes a picture of him. Then she immediately texts it to AppleLean. Taken by surprise, Junk Food Junkie immediately turns around and runs down the street.

Gabby continues her walk over to AppleLean's house. They're going to the County Fair today with Gabby's closest friends known as The Bunch.

Meanwhile, back in Junkieville. . .

The Munchies are all sitting around Junk Food Junkie, listening to the story of how he met Gabby Grape. There's Freddie French Fry, Junk Food Junkie's best friend, who is very loyal to him. He is also very fidgety and sneaky. Then there's Fats Goodie who is greedy, overweight, selfish and unkind. And there's Tuff Cookie. She is mean, rude, selfish, and very disrespectful. And lastly, there is Sammy Soda Pop. He is cold-hearted, bold and smart. "So, I meet this Gabby Grape character", says Junk Food Junkie. "She goes on and on and on about how important it is to eat PLENTY of fruits and vegetables every day. She says that apples are rich in fiber and that fiber helps you to do the Number Two!" (They all burst out laughing).

"TMI if you ask me", says Freddie French Fry. "Anyway, I offered her one of my delicious, chocolate chip cookies and she turned it down! "No thanks", she said. "I don't eat sugary snacks before dinner!" (They all burst out laughing again). "Oh yeah? Who told her that?" they ask. "Her parents!" he replies. They all say… "Yeesh!"

Gabby Grape is to Receive the Key to Healthyville

Gabby Grape and The Bunch are briskly walking to the County Fair. There's AppleLean who is wild, silly, playful and is very loyal to Gabby Grape. "Oh Gabby, aren't you excited? Today is the day Mayor Bloomfield is presenting you with the Key to Healthyville!" says AppleLean.

"OMG! It's so Grapey!" says Gabby. They all laugh. There's Brainy Broccoli who is smart, always happy and dependable. "Maybe I'll accept the Key for you, GG" he says with pride. Brainy Broccoli clears his throat, pretending to read an acceptance speech. "Thank you all for coming. I accept this award on behalf of all the citizens of Healthyville!" They all laugh again. And there's Wendy Bread who is adventurous, lively, funny and sometimes a little stubborn. Lastly, there is Mighty Milk who is strong, brave, zany and charming.

They're just about to reach the County Fair when Junk Food Junkie and his Munchies are coming around the corner. "Well, look who we have here", says Junk Food Junkie. "It's 'Ms. Purple Blob' and her goofy friends!" They all laugh hysterically. "Where are you all headed to in such a hurry?" "We're going to the County Fair" blurts out Brainy Broccoli. "Gabby Grape is getting the Key to Healthyville". "Be quiet, Brainy Broccoli!" says Applelean. "Oh, it's OK AppleLean" says GG. "As a matter of fact, they can come along with us if they like". (Again, Junk Food Junkie and his Munchies all laugh hysterically). "I wouldn't go ANYWHERE with you bunch of misfits!"

He turns to The Munchies and says "Let's say we have a little fun!" "Well, I am getting a little thirsty, J" says Sammy Soda Pop. "Why don't we make some fruit juice out of Gabby Grape!" "That sounds good", says Tuff Cookie. "Oh yeah, oh yeah!" says Fats Goodie. "No", says Junk Food Junkie. "I've got a better idea. You misfits go on ahead to the County Fair. We'll 'catch up' with you later. 'Ketchup' – get it? Ha! Ha! Ha!"

"GG, I think we better keep a close watch on him and his Munchies", says Mighty Milk. "I don't trust them!" "Awww, don't worry about those guys", says GG. "Let's just chill, relax and enjoy the Fair. Come on, Bunch! Today, I'm getting the Key to Healthyville!" They all laugh and give each other a friendly slap on the back.

As Gabby Grape and The Bunch walk away, Junk Food Junkie reveals his cruel idea to The Munchies. "Yep, I've got the PERFECT plan for Gabby Grape". "What's your plan, J?" asks Sammy Soda Pop. "We're going to set up a funny booby trap for Gabby Grape. This is going to be just so cool! Have you ever seen that booth at the County Fair where you throw a baseball at a target to make a clown fall into the water? Well, we'll fix the stage floor so it will open right under her just when the Mayor gives her the Key. She will fall right into a BIG TUB OF COLD WATER! Ha! Ha! Ha!

Yep, her getting the Key to Healthyville fits right into my plans! Ha! Ha! Ha! Ha!!!" "How do you suppose we do that?" asks Fats Goodie. "Right. None of us knows how to build stuff", says Tuff Cookie. Junk Food Junkie doesn't even hear them. He starts talking to himself instead, saying "Yes, the Mayor giving her the Key to Healthyville fits right into my plans. Ha! Ha! Ha! Ha! This is going to be fun!" The Munchies all look puzzled…

At the County Fair

GG and The Bunch stop by the Ping Pong Ball and Fish Bowl game. Wendy Bread steps up to play. She tosses ping pong balls at a table filled with rows of fish bowls. "Geez, Wendy! You missed every one of them!" jokes Mighty Milk. They all laugh. "Let a real 'Player' show you how to do it!" He misses them all, too, and they all laugh again. "Holy Blueberries! We'd better head on over to the main stage", says Gabby Grape. "Awww, come on GG. We have time to ride on one more ride - or maybe play just one more game?", asks Brainy Broccoli. "Maybe next time, my friend. Right now I have to talk to the Mayor about my acceptance speech. I'll meet you at the main stage".

On the way to the County Fair, Junk Food Junkie with his Munchies stop over to see Spud, Freddy French Fry's cousin. They pick up a few tools and a large water tub.

After arriving at the County Fair, they go to the main stage where no one has gathered yet. They go around the back and enter a door leading to the area beneath the stage. They immediately start taking the tools out of a bag. "How do you turn this thing on?" asks Fats Goodie. "Turn it on? It's a hammer! You don't turn it on. Jeez!" barks Freddy French Fry. "Oh, so you do this?" Fats begins to swing the hammer and hits Freddie French Fry in the head. "Gimme that thing before you hurt someone!" says Sammy Soda Pop. Sammy turns to Junk Food Junkie. "I don't know, J. I don't think this is such a good idea after all", says Sammy. "Don't worry, Sammy. It'll be a cinch," says Junk Food Junkie with a very sly laugh. He then looks around for where he can plug in an electric saw he got from Spud's house.

Gabby Grape sees the Mayor over in the food vendor's court. "Hello, Mayor Bloomfield!" He is eating a big, juicy veggie burger. With his mouth full, he says "Hello there, GG. Are you excited about getting the Key to Healthyville?" "Yes sir. I'd like to go over my speech with you. But first, Mayor Bloomfield, did I ever tell you the story about …? "Excuse me, GG. I shouldn't talk with my mouth full." He takes another bite, real quick – and then suddenly. Varoom! "Did you hear that loud sound?" asks the Mayor. "Yes, Mayor, I did. It sounds like it's coming from over by the main stage area!" The Mayor says, "Yes, it does!" "Well, you stay here and finish your sandwich, Mayor. I'll go and check it out." "Ok, GG. I'll be over there just as soon as I finish this delicious veggie burger."

He takes another big bite while GG smiles, waves goodbye and heads right over to the main stage. Once she arrives, she sees The Bunch. "Do you guys hear that loud noise?" "Yes", replies AppleLean. "We were just getting ready to investigate where the noise is coming from. It sounds like it's coming from behind the stage". "Follow me", says GG. They all walk behind the stage.

They look around and GG says, "It's coming from UNDER the stage!" They all enter the door under the stage and there they discover Junk Food Junkie and The Munchies busy at work cutting a hole in the stage floor.

Gabby Grape reaches into her secret pouch and takes a sip of her Super Grape Juice which gives her super strength! Then, in a whirlwind, she grabs Junk Food Junkie and The Munchies and ties them up with her Super Grapevine that she also keeps in her pouch!

Gabby Grape picks up the hammer and some loose nails lying around on the ground and fixes the hole in the stage floor and then hurries to take her seat on the stage next to the Mayor; the Bunch runs to their seats in the first row.

After a few words to the crowd by the Mayor, he asks Gabby Grape to join him at the podium to receive the Key to Healthyville! The crowd applauds wildly with glee.

She begins her acceptance speech. "Hello, good citizens of Healthyville. In accepting this award, it's important to know that I'm not suggesting you shouldn't eat fast foods or even junk foods. What I'm advising is that you eat them in moderation, which means cutting down on the amount of these foods that you eat! They contain fat, salt and sugar. Include more of the healthier foods like fruits, vegetables, grains and nuts. These are the real fast foods. And don't forget, you should exercise at least 3-5 times a week! Find a fun exercise that you love to do by yourself or with a friend. If you enjoy it, chances are you will do it often. Well, that's all I have to say. Oh, thanks for coming!!!" Colorful balloons are released as Gabby returns to her seat, floating high into the sky.

Meanwhile, under the stage, Junk Food Junkie has untied himself but not The Munchies! LOL. He has heard everything that is going on above him on the stage - he is furious and starts jumping up and down in rage. He is stomping his feet in anger! "Yes, Gabby Grape, my plans were foiled this time and you've won the 1st round! But trust me, there will be a 2nd round! I will return! Ha! Ha! Ha! Ha! Ha!!!

Gabby Grape and friends walk away.

The End

Gabby's Message

"I'm not suggesting that you shouldn't eat fast food or junk food. What I'm advising is that you eat them in moderation. This means cutting down on the amount of these foods that you eat. They contain fat, salt and sugar. Include more of the healthier foods like fruits, vegetables, grains and nuts. These are the real fast foods! Remember, "Grapes are Mother Nature's candy!"

Mensaje de Gabby

No estoy sugiriendo que usted no debe comer comida rápida o comida basura. Lo que estoy aconsejando es que los coma con moderación. Esto significa reducir la cantidad de estos alimentos que usted come. Contienen grasa, sal y azúcar. Incluya más de los alimentos más saludables, como frutas, verduras, granos y nueces. Estos son los verdaderos comidas rápidas! Recuerde, "Las uvas son caramelos de la madre naturaleza!"

www.ingramcontent.com/pod-product-compliance
Lightning Source LLC
Chambersburg PA
CBHW041644070526

44586CB00004B/74